COUNT ON YOUR FINGERS
AFRICAN STYLE

Count On Your Fingers African Style

Library of Congress Cataloging Number 96-086324
ISBN: 0-86316-250-9

Published by **Writers and Readers Publishing, Inc.**
for **Black Butterfly Books**

Printed in Hong Kong

A Note from the Author

PEOPLE ALL OVER THE WORLD COUNT ON THEIR FINGERS. Perhaps you do, too. People in Africa, as well as other places, have special ways of finger counting. In this book you will read about some of these ways.

If you were to go to Africa tomorrow, you would find that some people use finger counting, while others do not. Many people count on their fingers because it is their custom. They may say the number words and at the same time make signs with their fingers. People learn the finger signs that are right for their own languages. They know which sign is correct for each number.

More than a thousand languages are spoken in Africa. People who speak different languages meet in the marketplace. They can use finger signs to show "How much" and "How many," as you will learn in this book.

In school, children speak the language that is common to their region. Often it is different from the language they learned at home. In parts of East Africa the common language is Swahili, an African language. In other places it may be another African language, or Portuguese, French, English, or Arabic. As more people learn to speak these common languages, they may no longer use finger signs to discuss numbers in the market.

Each year more and more African children attend schools that are very much like yours. In school, they learn ways that are different from those of their parents. When I was in Africa I asked many students how their people counted on their fingers. Some knew very well how to do it. Others said, "I will ask my father" or "I will ask my grandmother."

Probably nothing will ever replace finger counting entirely. After all, fingers make such a handy calculator—they are always with you!

—Claudia Zaslavsky

You are in East Africa.
Today is a market day.
People come from near and far to
buy all sorts of things—food,
cloth, pots, beads.
Market day is a great event.

People meet friends they have
not seen for many days.
Some tell funny stories. Others have
sad news to give their friends.
People speak in excited voices
as they buy and sell.
Everyone tries to get the best price.
Some people are waving
their fingers as they speak.

You join the crowd.
An orange would taste good
on a hot day like this.
You decide to buy three so
you can keep two for later.

But how can you say that you
want three oranges?
You speak only English.
You don't hear anyone
speaking English.
Well, what can you do?

You can use your fingers.
You can point to the oranges and show
three on your fingers.
But how will you do it?
This way . . .

or some other way?
Go to the orange seller
and see what happens.

It works!
She gives you three oranges.
Now she asks you for *itatu* pennies—
one penny for each orange.

This is how the Kamba people
show three on their fingers.

Three Maasai boys are looking
at the oranges.
They talk to one another and laugh.
One boy shows this sign
with his right hand.
How many oranges does he want?
The market woman gives him
three oranges, too.

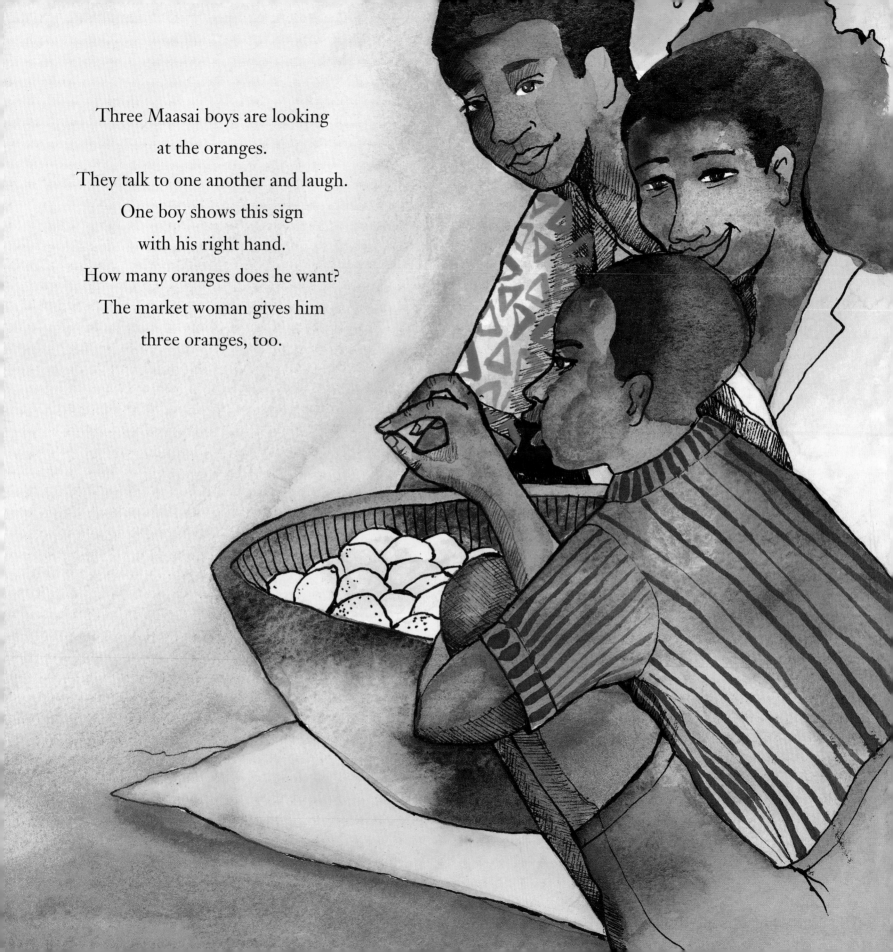

The Kamba people and the Maasai people
live near each other in
a country called Kenya.
The Maasai buy things like pots
and knives from the Kamba.

The Kamba buy cows and beads from the Maasai.
But they speak different languages.
They can say how many they want
and how much money to pay
with finger counting.

Now you see
some ripe yellow bananas.
The Kamba farmer picked them
just this morning.
How can you show
that you want eight bananas?
This way . . .

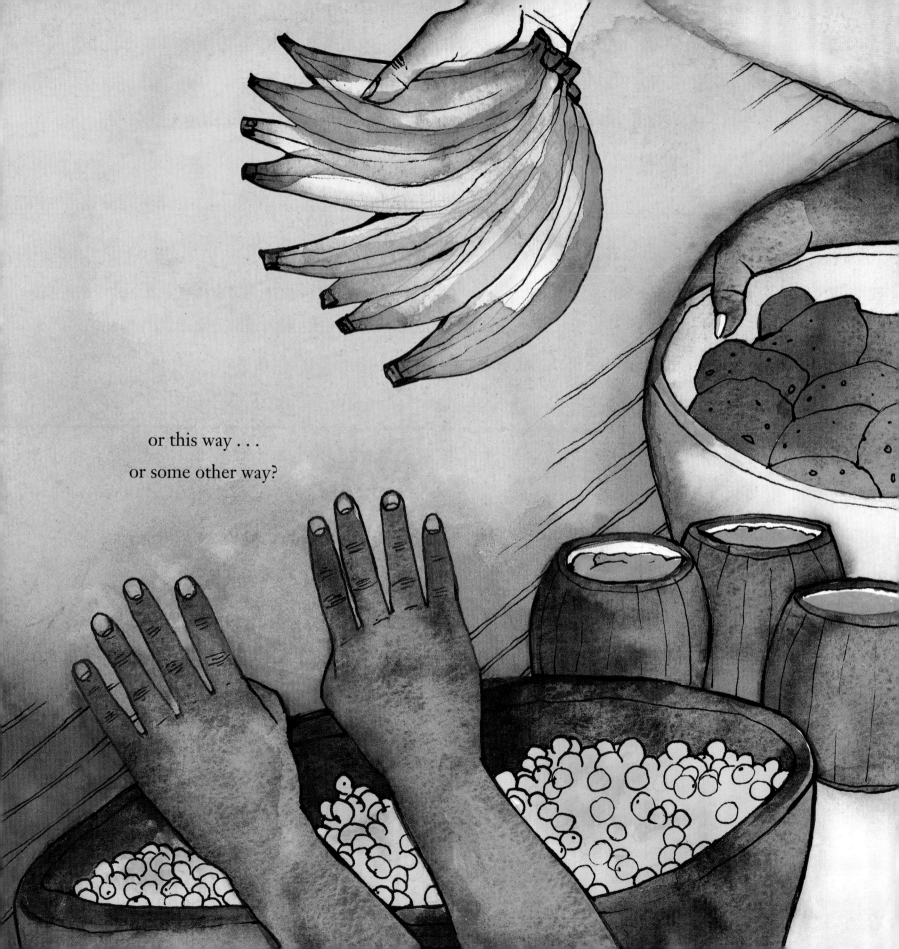

or this way . . .

or some other way?

This is the Kamba sign for eight.
The right hand holds three fingers
of the left hand.
Five fingers on the right and
three fingers on the left make eight.
The Kamba word for eight is *nyaanya*.

The Taita people also live in Kenya.
From his farm this Taita farmer
can see Mount Kilimanjaro,
the tallest mountain in Africa.
The Taita sign for three is just
like the Kamba sign.
The Taita word for three is *idadu*.
The Kamba word is *itatu*.

Can you guess what number
the Taita farmer is showing?

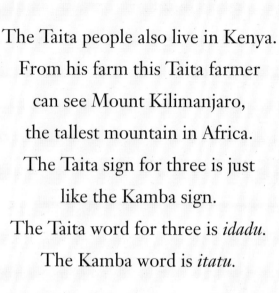

It is the Taita sign for eight.
Four fingers and four fingers
make eight.
The Taita word for eight is *inyanya*
It means four and four.

What beautiful beads!
The Maasai women make these
colorful necklaces while
the men and boys take
care of the cattle.

The man wants you to buy one.
How many shillings does he ask for it?
He waves the four fingers
of his right hand.
What can he mean?

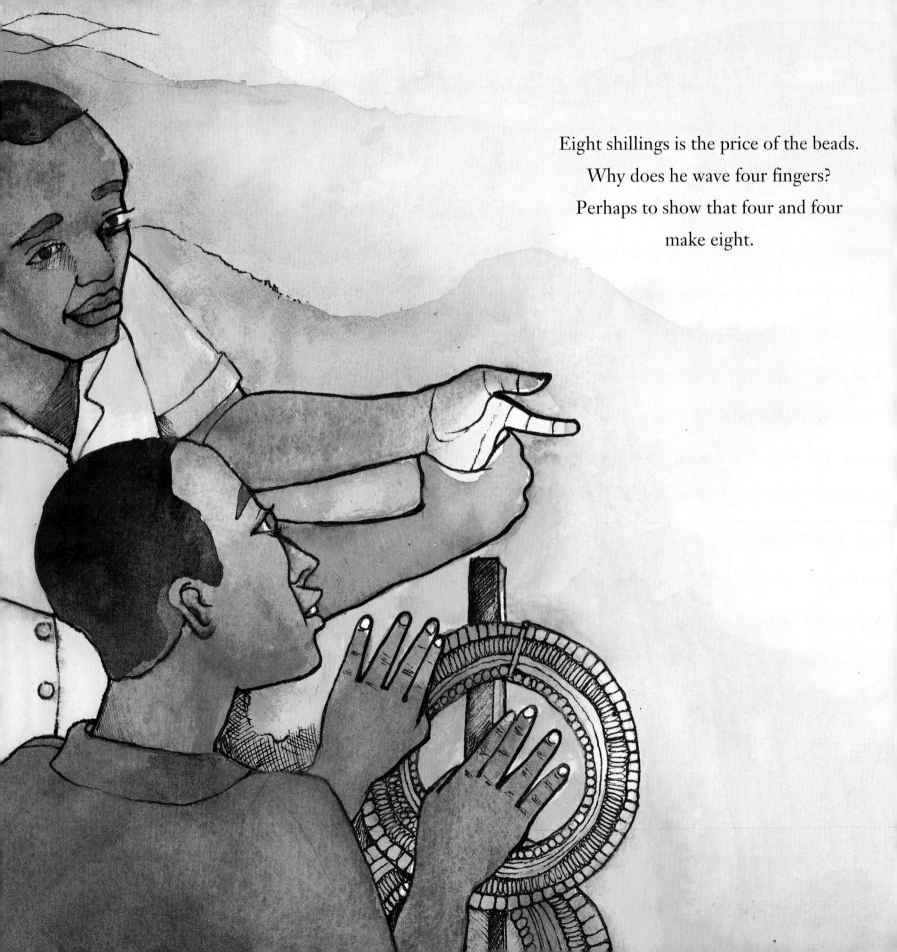

Eight shillings is the price of the beads.
Why does he wave four fingers?
Perhaps to show that four and four
make eight.

All these people live in the
same country in East Africa—
Kamba, Taita, Maasai.
They all live in Kenya.
Yet they all have
different ways of showing eight
on their fingers.

Very small children
in Africa play
finger games and
learn to count
on their fingers.
Didn't you?
Did you say:

"This little pig went to market.

This little pig stayed at home.

This little pig ate roast beef.

This little pig had none.

This little pig cried all the way home."

Little children in Africa learn finger games from their big brothers and sisters.

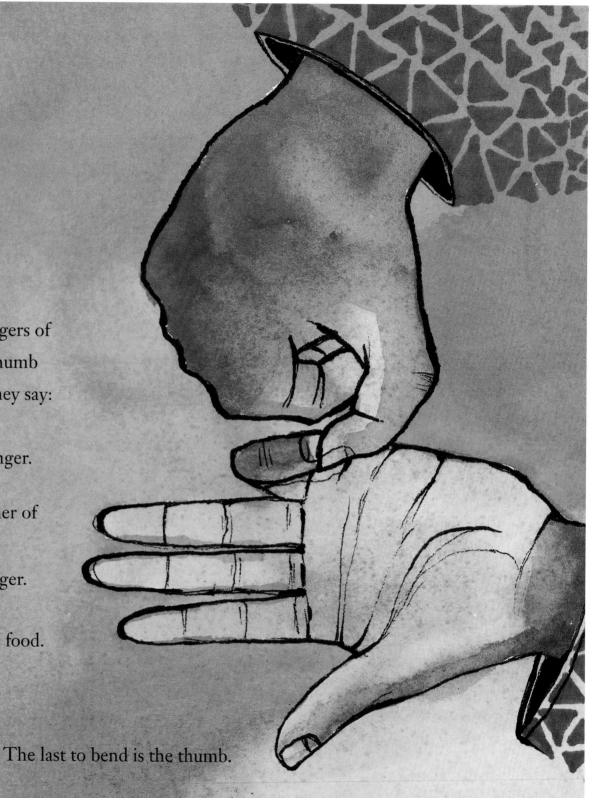

Children bend the fingers of
one hand with the thumb
of the other hand as they say:

"This is the little finger.

This is the big brother of
the little finger.

This is the long finger.

This one picks up the food.

The last to bend is the thumb.

Here is the story of the fingers that cry out:

"Nye! Nye! Nye!"

"What's the matter?"

"He's hungry!"

"The food is in the pot."

"Let's eat it!"

"When Mommy comes home, I'll tell!"

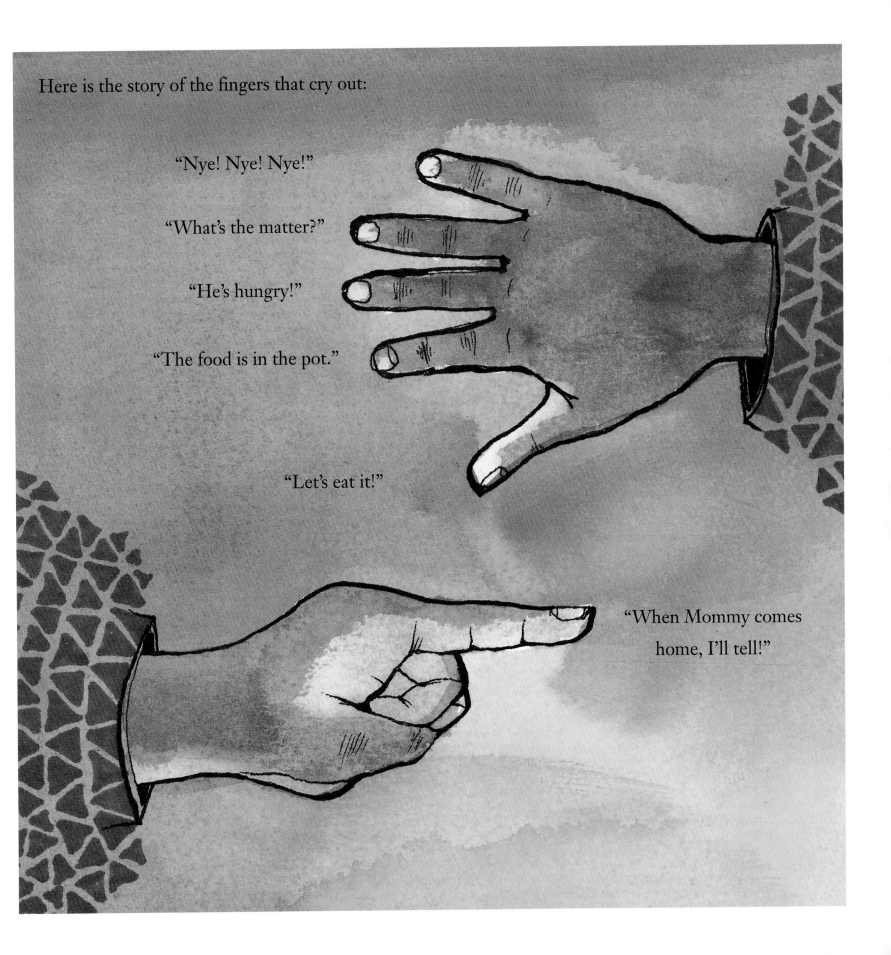

All over the world
children and grown-ups
sometimes use their
fingers for counting.
Don't you?

Fatu can show you her way . . .
Fatu lives in Sierra Leone,
a country in West Africa.
Often she helps her mother sell
bright red tomatoes.
She calls out:
"Tomatoes! Fresh tomatoes!"

Fatu has twenty tomatoes
in her basin.
Her mother laid them down
as Fatu counted them
on her fingers.
She bent one finger
for each tomato.
To count from one to five,
she bent the fingers of her left hand,
starting with the little finger.

Then she counted from six to ten
on her right hand, starting
with the little finger.
For eleven to twenty
she did the same thing all over again.

Some of Fatu's people
may have counted from
eleven to twenty on their toes.
Her people, the Mende,
have a special word for twenty.
It is *nu gboyongo*.
It means a whole person.
It means that all ten fingers and
all ten toes have been counted.

Fatu's mother does not need
to count on her fingers.
She can do even
the biggest sums in her head.
Fatu will be able to do that too
when she is older.

Do you know that some of our English
number words are named
for finger counting?
Eleven means one left.
Count out all ten fingers.
Then you will need one more
to reach eleven.
Twelve means two left over,
after counting all ten fingers.

Many people in South Africa show six
by holding up the right thumb.

The Zulu people live in South Africa.
Isithupa is the Zulu word for six.
It means take the thumb.
Isishiyagalombili means
to leave out two fingers.
Can you guess what number that is?

It is the Zulu word for eight.
The word tells how many fingers
are not used.

People all over the world
count on their fingers.
Their number names prove it!!

Can you make up your own finger signs for
the numbers from one to ten?
Ask your friends to guess
which numbers you are showing.
Then make up new number names
to go with your signs.